Homemade Dog Treats and

Homemade Dog Food

35 Homemade Dog Treats and Homemade Dog Food Recipes
and Information to Keep Man's Best Friend Happy, Healthy, and
Disease Free

By: Brittany Boykin

Homemade Dog Treats and Homemade Dog Food

Published by CAC Publishing LLC.

ISBN 978-0-9987140-2-8 paperback

ISBN 978-1-948489-73-7 eBook

You're about to discover deliciously healthy meals to keep your best friend happy, healthy and disease free! If you love this book and your dog loves the recipes, I would be extremely grateful if you could leave a review on Amazon. Reviews are the best way to help your fellow readers distinguish good books from bad so make sure to help them out! You can leave your review by Clicking Here

If you're interested in learning how to train your dog, make sure to check out my book 'The Dog Training Bible.' It's a great book with lots of training tips for dogs of all ages! You can check it out HERE

Contents

Introduction

If you're like most people, then your dog is a true member of your family. Just as you'd want to be sure your family members are getting good healthy, nutritious food, you want to be sure your dog is getting the same.

Many commercial canned dog foods contain preservatives and additives that are not always considered safe for human use. If you wouldn't feed them to your children, why would you feed them to your dog?

While making homemade dog food is often healthier and can be cheaper than buying commercial dog food, there are several foods that you shouldn't include in any dog recipes if you plan to make homemade dog food.

Dogs have very simplified digestive systems compared to ours. This means that some combinations of human foods can cause stomach upsets, illness, nerve damage, seizures, or even death. There is a section on foods to avoid feeding your dog later in this book.

Keep in mind that when you're creating your own homemade dog food, your dog doesn't need nearly as much protein as you might believe. Some people try to feed their dog bones or meat off-cuts, but your dog will still need things added to his or her diet to promote good health. A good balance of carbohydrates and some vegetables will be important to keep up energy levels, but avoid adding potato as it may cause digestive problems in some breeds.

You should also remember that some larger breeds of dog, such as German Shepherds, are susceptible to bloat (gastric digestive torslon or gastric digestive vulvulus, which can result in a very painful and sudden death). It's important not to include any ingredients that could potentially expand inside the stomach after eating, so be sure to overcook any rice or pasta until it's completely expanded before feeding to avoid this potentially fatal condition. You should also try to feed larger breeds twice daily rather than one large meal to help avoid bloat from occurring.

The recipes in this book are the ones I've been using for my two show-standard German Shepherd dogs for years. Both dogs have won multiple awards and have always displayed a fine shiny coat. They both also have healthy teeth and good bone growth. All of the recipes in this book were approved by their vet (prior to feeding any of these recipes to your dog I strongly suggest you double check with your vet as well).

Once you begin making your own dog food and realize how easy it is, and how little time it can take, you'll never go back to feeding your dog sloppy, mysterious commercial food again.

Choosing the right dog food is probably the most important decision you'll ever make for your dog. Whether your dog is a puppy or a senior, their diet is one of the most important aspects of their overall health and well-being. Dog food nutrition impacts every facet of your dog's life. Like how fast puppies grow, their behavioral patterns, their physical appearance, etc. are all directly linked to the nutrition their owners provide.

The Key Benefits of a Healthy and Nutritious Dog Food Plan

A nutritious and well-balanced dog food plan promotes:

• A healthier coat

• Stronger muscles and more developed bones

• Brighter, clearer eyes

• More solid stool (Which can be nice if you live in an apartment complex and have to pick up after your dog)

• Better dental health

• Less digestive upsets

• Bursts of energy

• Fewer behavioral problems

• A longer, healthier Life

That's basically every aspect of their lives. Think about it in a human sense, when we go on diets and eat fresh, unprocessed foods, we feel ten times better, right? We notice an increase in energy levels, more consistent bathroom schedules, hair and nails can grow faster and look healthier, etc. It's exactly the same with your dog!

Chapter 1: What's Wrong with Commercial Dog Food?

With the ever-growing uncertainty about what's actually inside most commercial dog foods, it's no wonder organic dog food is growing in popularity. The closed loop of so many dog food industry secrets is enough to make even the most trusting of people alarmed by what we're actually feeding our beloved dogs.

In recent years, the dog food industry has improved labeling of ingredients being put into most commercial dog foods to some degree. Labels will tell you what percentage of the total product is protein, whether cereal, bran, grain, rice or vegetables have been added, and what additives and preservatives are in the can.

Unfortunately, this doesn't always tell you what kind of meat is included in the meat section of the labeling. It may not even tell you clearly what kinds of fillers are used to bulk out the food inside the can. These can sometimes include cereals that may not always agree with a dog's digestive system.

When you read the label, you should begin to realize that you could be feeding your dog a cocktail of chemicals, additives and preservatives designed to increase the shelf-life of the dog food product and enhance flavor and appearance. These extra chemicals are not designed to increase or enhance your dog's life or health.

Even commercial kibble and dry dog food contains very high amounts of chemical preservatives, artificial colors and flavors along with other additives.

The decision to feed your pet all-natural, home-made dog foods means you're offering your dog the best chance of a healthy life. You dog will have a reduced risk of contracting many of the diseases directly linked to the addition of so many chemicals in commercial products.

Chapter 2: Feeding Your Dog

To sustain your dog's good health, it's vital to feed him/her a well-balanced diet and the correct amount of food every day. There is a wide variety of canine foods available, so it can be hard deciding which one is the most beneficial choice for your pet. There are, however, particular dietary nutrients that a dog can't do without - protein, carbohydrates, fat, vitamins, minerals, fiber, and water, not to mention the age, health and lifestyle factors to consider, and this helps to make the task of picking out the most suitable diet less difficult.

Diet Plan

Dogs are omnivorous in their feeding habits and can be kept satisfactory on specially designed vegetarian diet programs, although they do prefer meat-based meals. In a wild state the dog hunts, kills, feeds, then rests. He may stuff himself on a whole animal one day, and then go without food for the following two or three; this is why a lot of dogs are keen to eat until they're fit to burst - intuition tells them they may have to hold out some time before their next meal.

Adult domestic dogs are often fed once a day, but dividing that feed into two meals adds relationship and interest. It's also preferable to feed certain deep-chested breeds, like German Shepherds, Great Danes, and Setters, several small meals as opposed to one big one, to avoid potentially terminal digestive conditions such as bloat.

You will find retail produced clinical diets available, typically only obtainable from veterinarians, that can assist dogs struggling with a wide range of disease, like kidney stones, signs of senility, obesity, digestive disturbances, diabetes, mellitus and tooth and gum problems. There are even food items engineered for long-coated breeds, in addition to life-stage formulas. You may also choose from holistic diets that incorporate no synthetic additives and diets designed for allergy sufferers.

Required Nutrients

Usually, dogs aren't difficult to feed, and they thrive on a diet not really different to humans, albeit with a little more protein. The majority of foods of animal origin, cereal products, root vegetables and fats are easy for them to break down. The trick of correct feeding is to give a balanced diet that provides all essential goodness in the appropriate proportions to one another with the objective intended - work, breeding, growth or health adulthood. These types of nutrients are listed below:

Carbohydrates

Carbohydrates, by means of cooked cereal starch or sugar, should be around 15-20% by weight of the dog's food (after taking away any water present) or about one-fifth of the calories. Dog biscuits, pasta and rice are three useful energy foods for dogs, and rice is a useful food item for canines allergic to wheat.

Proteins

Proteins within meat and plants (although the latter is substandard to the former) improve body tissue, carry out "repairs" and produce hormones. The majority should come from animal foods (meat and dairy products), or high-quality vegetable protein like soya.

Minerals

Minerals are occasionally referred to as "ash" on dog-food labels. The essential ones are calcium, phosphorus and sodium chloride (common salt) in a well-balanced combination. Calcium and phosphorus constitute most of the mineral matter of bone and must be utilized at the rate of about 3% calcium/phosphorus in the diet; an excessive amount of calcium in the diet, particularly in large-breed puppies, can result in skeletal irregularities, while an excessive amount of phosphorus (found in high meat and offal diets) could potentially cause eclampsia in lactating female dogs.

Additional essential minerals for good health, like zinc and copper, occur naturally in meat, cereals as well as other components of a balanced diet.

Vitamins

Vitamin A (also called retinol) is important for growth and eyesight, while vitamins of the B group are crucial for the upkeep, in particular, of the nervous system.

Vitamin D assists the body create calcium, required for healthy bones and teeth, as is phosphorus. Vitamin E (tocopherol) is important for the leveling of cell membranes. Since canines can create their own vitamin C (ascorbic acid, essential for maintaining healthy connective tissue and skin), this doesn't necessarily have to be part of the diet.

Fat

Fat contributes to food palatability, but is in fact only essential as a source of the essential fatty acids (EFAs, also known as polyunsaturates) which are vital to maintain body health. They work mainly by handling water loss through the skin. A deficiency in EFAs can lead to reproductive, skin, coat and wound therapeutic problems.

Fiber

An absence of fiber in the diet may result - particularly in elderly, inactive dogs - in bowel problems and other digestive problems cause by sluggish bowels. Fiber is provided through the indigestible plant matter in foods like cooked and raw veggies as well as cereals.

Balancing Act

It's critical that the balance of nutrients provided to a dog is correct, since excesses could cause as many health issues as inadequacies. If your dog gets more calories each day than his body requires, he will get fat. Just as in humans, obesity accounts for many canine illnesses, like heart problems, joint ailments and decline in lung function.

Here is a general guideline balance for some of the required nutrients in a dog's diet:

• 50-60% Protein – animal meat, seafood, eggs or dairy

• 10% Carbohydrates – grains and beans

• 40-50% Vegetables

• Fat – from oil or meat

• Calcium – crushed or powdered egg shells; a supplement

• Fatty acids – cooked egg yolks, oatmeal, plant oils and other foods

How Much Should I Feed My Dog?

This depends on a few factors specific to your dog:

1. Size and Weight

2. Age

3. Level of Activity

4. Personality

5. The Outside Temperature

Young puppies and active working dogs may require more food (calories) per day than the average pooch; while an old, inactive dog will need less.

Here is the standard feeding chart that's typically provided on most dog food bags for reference.

Weight of Dog	Amount of Food Per Day
5 pounds	1/2 cup to 5/8 cup
10 pounds	3/4 cup to 1 cup
20 pounds	1 1/4 cups to 1 3/4 cups
40 pounds	2 1/4 cups to 3 cups
60 pounds	3 cups to 4 cups
80 pounds	3 2/3 cups to 5 cups
100 pounds	4 1/4 cups to 6 cups

Keeping Track of the Calories

Energy is calculated in units of heat called calories. In a healthy dog, the amount of calories he requires levels out the number of calories that his body uses daily. If this balance is well kept, the dog stays healthy and fit and his weight remains regular. An underfed dog steadily loses weight and condition as his body pulls on the reserves of fat and protein to make up the insufficiencies in his diet.

The amount of calories a dog needs daily is dependent on multiple factors such as: his size, life stage, activity level and individuality. As an example, a little healthy adult dog with two hours of regular activity a day demands anything between 125 and 700 calories daily depending on his size; a big dog will need from 1,400 per day, depending on size.

Puppies require more calories with regards to their body weight due to their rapid growth, tend to be more susceptible to heat loss because of their small size, and their energy requirements are greater. Lactating female dogs require some 50 to 60% more calories than usual, and highly active (working) dogs require at least 40% more calories than normal moderately energetic requirements.

When Should I Feed My Dog?

Most owners feed either in the morning or the evening, and quite often both, determined by their dog's age needs or individual preferences. Some canines fare better with their daily ration broken into two or even three meals, while some are pleased to eat their daily allowance in just a single helping, providing it's safe for them to do so.

It's best to not feed adult dogs at the same periods each day, since counting on a rigid routine can upset the dog if you come home late and aren't able to give him food at the predicted time. Being unsure of when they will be fed actually helps keep a dog food-orientated, which often proves most helpful when training; additionally, it discourages fussy eating.

Feeding Recommendations

Here are a few basic guidelines to adhere to when feeding your dog:

• Place a feeding mat, or newspaper, under feeding bowls, since many canines are sloppy eaters.

• It is advisable to introduce changes to diet little by little to prevent intestinal problems.

• Never give spiced food or that to which any liquor has been added.

• To avoid choking, get rid of all bones from fresh meats and fish.

• Fresh, clean drinking water must always be accessible.

• Make certain food and water bowls are always clean.

• By no means allow your dog to consume chocolate intended for human consumption, as it's toxic to them.

• Confer with your vet if your dog exhibits any reluctance to eat or drink.

• Dissuade your dog from begging at the table, and definitely don't give into it (no matter how cute they look).

Food Types

Good-quality proprietary food is the simplest to feed. It consists of all the essential nutrients in the correct proportions, which includes vitamins and minerals that may be lacking from a home-made diet of fresh or cooked meat and table scraps.

These are four types of commercially prepared food:

1. Wet or Moist Canned or Pouch Dog Food

Canned food has high water content and is available in a wide array of flavors. It's typically the preferred choice of dogs.

Pros:

• Extremely palatable

• Contains all the nutrients a dog needs

• Long storage time if unopened

Cons:

• Bulky to store and heavy to carry

• Fattening

• Strong odor

• Not good for teeth

• Contains many artificial additives

• Spoils quickly

• Expensive

2. Semi-moist Pouch Dog Food

Often containing vegetable protein like soya, this food type contains less water than canned, therefore keeps well in a bowl without drying out and losing texture.

Pros:

• Palatable

• Contains all the nutrients a dog needs

• Easier to store than the cans

Cons:

• Fattening

• Strong odor

• Not good for teeth

• Very expensive

• Contains man-made artificial additives

• Spoils quickly

3. Dry Complete Dog Food

As its name suggests, dry complete food contains minimal water and all the nutrients your dog needs. Some types are designed to be moistened with water before feeding, while other types can be fed as they are, in which case your dog will need plenty of water to drink in conjunction with it.

Pros:

• Economical

• Low odor

• Contains all the nutrients a dog needs

• Better for teeth

Cons:

• Bulky to store

• Not as palatable as canned/semi-moist

• High cereal content can cause problems for gluten-sensitive dogs

4. Dry Complementary Dog Food

Designed to be fed with canned, cooked or raw meat, this food usually comprises cereal meal or biscuits. Fed alone, it doesn't fulfill a dog's daily nutritional needs.

Pros:

• Economical

- Low odor

- Good source of energy

- Most are supplemented with vitamins and minerals

- Better for teeth

Cons:

- Time-consuming to mix with protein-giving ingredients

- Spoils if stored too long

- Bulky to store

Foods to Avoid Feeding Your Dog

Many people feed their dogs with human foods, either from table scraps or as a treat. Others mistakenly believe that feeding your dog with food that humans love is also a way to show how much you love them. Your loving gestures could actually be harming your dog.

Unfortunately many of the foods we would see as treats may cause injury and damage internal organs. Spoiling your dog with a little treat could even be jeopardizing your dog's life.

Dogs are also notorious for getting into garbage and eating whatever they can find. Try to dispose of any garbage securely to minimize the risk of your dog eating something that could be potentially harmful.

Here is a list of foods to *AVOID* feeding your dog:

Alcohol: Alcohol can cause altered breathing, diarrhea, vomiting, abnormal blood acidity, coma and even death.

Avocado: Avocado contains "persin," which is known to cause diarrhea and vomiting.

Bones: Feeding a dog any type of bones, whether cooked or raw, can cause obstructions within the digestive system. The sharp shards of bone passing through the intestines or bowel may also cause lacerations. Look for larger marrowbones that are much less likely to splinter or cause internal damage.

Corn on the Cob: Feeding a dog a corn cob can cause painful intestinal blockages that will need to be removed surgically. Non-removal can cause death.

Chocolate: Chocolate can be toxic to a dog's heart and central nervous system, leading to seizures, convulsions and even heart attack. It can also cause vomiting and diarrhea.

Coffee: Coffee contains caffeine which can damage the nervous system and cause the heart rate to increase, which could result in heart attack.

Citrus: Citrus oil can cause vomiting in many dogs.

Fat Trimmings: Offering your dog the fat trimmings from any meat you're preparing can be one of the causes of pancreatitis. This is a very painful inflammation of the pancreas that could lead to death.

Fish: too much raw fish, canned fish or cooked fish can cause a thiamine deficiency in some dogs. Thiamine is a B vitamin, and a deficiency in this can cause loss of appetite and seizures. In very severe cases, it can cause death.

Garlic: Garlic can damage red blood cells in dogs, causing anemia.

Grapes: Grapes, currants and raisins contain a substance that is toxic to dogs that can damage kidneys, leading to renal failure.

Hops: Giving a dog beer made from hops can increase the heart rate, and cause high temperatures, fever and seizures.

Macadamia Nuts: Macadamia nuts contain a substance that is toxic to dogs that affects the nervous system and the digestive system. Symptoms could include muscle spasms, lack of coordination or collapse.

Milk: Excessive amounts of dairy products can cause diarrhea in some dogs.

Mushrooms: Mushrooms contain toxins that can seriously affect the nervous system and digestive system in dogs. Mushrooms may also cause a dog to go into shock, which can result in death.

Onions: Onions contain disulfides and sulfoxides that cause damage to red blood cells that could result in anemia.

Raw Eggs: There used to be a belief that feeding a dog raw egg would make their coats shine. This isn't true. Raw eggs contain an enzyme known as avidin which actively decreases the dog's ability to absorb vitamin B. Raw eggs may also contain salmonella.

Raw Meat: uncooked meat can contain bacteria that can cause diarrhea and vomiting.

Rhubarb Leaves: Rhubarb leaves are toxic to dogs, causing damage to the nervous system, the digestive system and the kidneys.

Rotten food: never feed a dog rotten or spoiled food, as it may contain bacteria and other toxins that can affect the digestive system, and cause vomiting and diarrhea.

Tobacco: Nicotine can have seriously damaging effects on the digestive and nervous systems that can cause rapid heart-beat and may result in collapse, coma and even death.

Yeast: Yeast dough can expand within a dog's stomach, which could lead to a rupture within the stomach or intestines.

Training Your Dog to Only Eat on Command

One of the easiest ways to protect your dog from eating something potentially harmful is to train him to only eat on command. This reduces the chance of your dog stealing a treat from the table or from an unattended BBQ. You will also find your dog is less likely to forage for food through the garbage.

Before you feed your dog, hold his bowl up above his nose and give him the command to sit. Once he's sitting, tell him to stay and place the bowl down in front of him.

If he moves before being released, reprimand him with a sharp "ah ah" sound and make him sit down again. When he's sitting, staying in position and waiting without rushing straight to the food, he will look to you for the command to eat. Tell him "okay" or "eat" or whatever command you want to give him.

This can take a couple of meals before your dog gets the idea, but he'll learn fast – especially if he wants his dinner!

Do NOT make the mistake of thinking this is teasing your dog, or being cruel in anyway. You're not. This is a very effective way to let your dog understand that you are the pack leader in your home and all food is only allowed and approved by you.

Your dog will begin to re-think stealing food if he knows the pack leader hasn't allowed it. This could be a very helpful way to make sure your dog isn't eating anything he shouldn't be!

Chapter 3: Homemade Dog Food

With all the recent news concerning dog food recalls and issues with commercial dog foods, the homemade dog food movement has really started catching on, and for good reason.

Planning and preparing your four legged friend's meals from scratch has multiple benefits, which includes complete control of all meals served. You know exactly what goes into every single meal and where the ingredients came from; in addition to the comfort of knowing that their food was prepared in a clean environment.

Much like coming up with a meal plan for yourself, it does require some organization to put together a homemade feeding plan for your dog, not to mention the time it takes to make all of the meals. The most common homemade dog foods include big meaty stews, healthy soups, and veggies. The homemade dog food route also has the added benefit of making nutritionally balanced meals and achieving the caloric demands for your dog. If you arm yourself with the right dog food recipes, the right program, and, of course, your veterinarian's approval, this practice isn't that hard to keep.

Ignore the restaurant doggy bag. Nowadays, more dogs are eating on their own patios, gulping down homemade canine food. There have been gradual rises in the number of people who are requesting help with creating homemade diets for their canines, according to majority of veterinarians in the US. The trend to homemade dog food started about a decade ago, and the vast majority of dog owners continue to feed their dogs commercial pet foods. The rise for homemade dog food got stronger after the spring 2007 recall of melamine-tainted pet food.

Apart from product contamination scares, numerous pet owners feel that homemade meals are a fresher option to ready-made pet food. There are also pet owners who have considerable time and have a quite strong bond with their pet and feel that if they're going to maintain a healthy diet, they want their dog to eat healthy, as well.

Owners may also prepare and cook for their pets as an expression of affection since most pet owners see their dogs as children.

Balanced Nutrition

So you're convinced to try home cooking for your pooch? What should you take into account before getting started?

Whether owners are getting recipes from a guide book, the net, or via their vet or veterinary nutritionist, one issue tops the list. Owners intend to make sure the recipe is going to supply something that is complete and balanced for their dog. From a nutritional perspective, that's the biggest obstacle that someone has when trying to feed homemade. There aren't any magic foods or ingredients for this.

Commercial pet foods are designed to provide sufficient nutrients, but dog owners who make homemade dog food must ensure that the diet includes a protein source, a carbohydrate source, sufficient vitamins and minerals, plus some fat. Dogs do have a necessity for a small amount of fat.

Home cooks can blend protein and carbohydrates in a variety of combinations, such as lamb and rice, beef and potatoes, or chicken and pasta. Carbs are an economical source of energy and supply some important amino acids and fatty acids.

Furthermore, a selection of vegetables would be perfectly suitable, even though vets caution towards onions and garlic, which can be poisonous to dogs.

Additional foods to protect your dogs from: raisins, grapes, macadamia nuts, chocolate, and raw meat, which unearths canines to risks, like salmonella and E. coli. All meat must be cooked properly.

Even though owners can find plentiful recipes for homemade dog food online and in books, some professionals encourage pet owners to take the recipes first to their vet and ask if their pet doctor could help them determine if it's balanced.

Moreover, owners doing homemade diets must have their dog and the diet assessed at least twice a year. Owners also need to remember that dogs in different life stages or with health disorders can have totally different dietary requirements than a normal, healthy adult canine.

Owners can also search for a reputable vet nutritionist to assist them produce a balanced diet. Often, these specialists are available through a close by vet school, or may be open to consult with your regular vet by means of phone or the web.

For pet owners who wish to find dog food recipes online, internet sites that are run by board-certified vets or veterinary nutritionists can be good sources.

Supplementation

Do dogs eating homemade dog food require supplementation to make certain they're getting sufficient nutrients? The answer is YES.

Though views differ significantly, it's a belief of many that a healthy dog's nutritional needs can be fulfilled with nothing more than food and exercise. Calcium supplements and Magnesium levels are often the only two deficiency considerations when feeding a homemade dog food recipe diet.

Specialists say nutritional inadequacies can result in health issues. Calcium is among the most common deficiency in a homemade diet plan that isn't professionally balanced. When canines don't get adequate calcium, they're vulnerable to a condition known as nutritional secondary hyperparathyroidism, which can result in soft bones and bone injuries.

Vets have seen these kinds of results on young dogs consuming unbalanced homemade diets. They see issues with their bone growth -- they're clearly not growing normally, thus you'll see bent limbs, or they're really bent and bowed. Sometimes, it may also be serious enough that they see actual broken bones.

You can boost calcium with unflavored yogurt, white cheese, pulverized egg shells, and sardines. Vitamin D to discharge the calcium can be acquired from cod liver oil or time spent outside, on a sunny day. Magnesium is found in kelp and spinach, which are both acceptable when steamed first.

Apart from calcium, other vitamins and minerals are crucial, too, such as magnesium, iron, and zinc. These nutrients need to be covered, which can be very tough for homemade dog food.

Canine owners must ask their vets with regard to supplementation.

Time and Expense

Needless to say, it's more time-consuming to cook than to buy commercial dog food at the store. As for expense, a lot will depend on the size of the dog.

Is there a variation in cost between store-bought and homemade pet food? Not really. If you decide to purchase high-quality and organic products for your homemade dog food, it'll be costly. If you opt to buy the best, premium brands of dog food in the store, it will likewise be pricey. If you choose your manufacturers or ingredients meticulously, you can lessen the cost of dog food. Above all, you shouldn't bargain the health and well-being of your pet.

It's completely your choice, as the owner, whether you choose to provide your dog homemade or store-bought food. If you opt to make any changes to your dog's present diet, you must ensure that you introduce new foods little by little to avoid diarrhea and digestive difficulties.

Large dogs like Saint Bernards and Rottweilers, for example, are more expensive to feed compared to small breeds. If you have a dog that's over 50 or 60 lbs. -- for instance, you have two or more of them -- obviously, the cost will be more, compared to the owner that has two tiny Yorkie.

It's also critical that owners stay thorough and strictly follow the suggested dietary formula. A lot of owners, as time passes, will make little alterations in the diet as a result of ease of cooking or price of ingredients, an event known as recipe drift. You should not make these changes without conferring with a vet, as they could trigger malnutrition.

Shelf-life and Storage

Packaged foods have a long shelf-life. Not so with homemade meals. It's an advantage that with homemade food you're opting for fresh ingredients; it's a disadvantage that you don't have a long shelf life.

For small dogs, owners can make a big batch, freeze it, and take out servings as required. This is going to last for some time. But meals for large canines are best kept in the refrigerator since it's most likely going to be gone in just a couple of days.

The important thing: Home-cooked diets can be very healthy and gratifying for owners, but demand a commitment of time and extra cost from the owner, and assessment with a vet to make sure the diet is not causing the dog harm.

Homemade Food Benefits

Which would you prefer for dinner - a microwaveable TV dinner or a homemade meal by your Mom? Just about everyone has eaten both, and has a personal preference. Odds are, whomever is making the homemade food can do a lot better than a frozen brick of "food." This situation may make it simpler to empathize with your canine when you fill his bowl with nuggets of processed meal and he looks up your with that facial expression that says, "you've got to be kidding me?"

Or perhaps, your furry best friend is more than willing to scarf down anything that gets in his bowl. If so, you may want to ask yourself, "Is traditional dog food the best thing for him?" Your dinner alternatives may well be a no-brainer, but finding the right option for your pet isn't usually that simple. He's counting on you to make the healthiest and best tasting decisions for him.

When you make food at home for your pet, you're guaranteed that your dog is eating foods that aren't packed full of the preservatives, additives, and chemicals that are often present in commercial dog foods. The big question is: is this enough to meet his daily nutritional requirements?

Various Kinds of Homemade Dog Food

Yes, there are various types of homemade dog food out there. Just like human food, homemade dog food can be classified to filter the search for your furry friend's best diet. But, lines may be blurred, and ideas can overlap. For example, you may decide to feed a raw dog food diet while staying away from all of the foods that specialists have deemed possibly damaging. Or you may choose to use holistic health concepts while using all organic and natural ingredients. That is what homemade dog food is centered on, after all - modifying your dog's diet in a manner that fulfills you both.

Raw Dog Food or Biologically Appropriate Raw Food (BARF)

Your dog is a wild animal that's been domesticated and, as with human beings, any species' best diet is its indigenous one. A dog's native diet is meat. Furthermore, some experts would attest that raw meat is ideal. Unlike human beings, dogs aren't usually prone to conditions like salmonella and e-coli.

Organic Homemade Dog Food

You'd have to be living under a rock if you've overlooked all of the fuss pertaining to organic foods. An entire bunch of people believe that bug killers, herbicides, human waste, sewage gunge, radiation, genetic changes, and synthetic additives have no place in or on our produce. But what about meat? Are you aware that your meat, and the meat that you prepare for your pet, can be organic and natural as well?

Organic meat is farmed from animals that have been grown devoid of synthetic growth hormones or medicines, and have not been fed animal by-products. Organic and natural foods provide no more nourishment than conventional ones, but their appeal is strictly about what's NOT inside them. You'll be spending more for less though, but it's much less of what you don't want and don't need. Most grocery stores carry organic meat nowadays so finding them shouldn't be a problem.

Homemade Holistic Dog Food

Holistic feeding approaches and medicine are based upon the concept that feeding the mind and body assists in regaining and managing health and vigor. Principles consist of ideals like balance and assortment. Holistic diets may be given raw or cooked - your decision.

Meal rotation and assortment is important to holistic health principles, just like variety is vital to your own good diet regime. Holistic dog food followers believe that grains are acceptable for dogs - in line with the premise that when dogs eat wild animals, they likewise ingest the contents of the stomach of those animals, which includes grains and greens. Many holistic dog food recipes are positioned around two parts protein, one part carbohydrates, and one part veggies. Using these guidelines, you are able to create a variety of recipes.

Should You Cook For Your Dog?

Not surprisingly, you may feel stressed out at the notion of feeding your dog from your own kitchen. Perhaps you have little time to cook even for your own human family. Try using the following time-saving suggestions to make your dog's improved wellness and longevity achievable:

• Instead of dicing fresh veggies, keep bags of frozen ones readily available.

• Instead of pureeing veggies, make use of prepared baby food.

• Prepare meals ahead of time and freeze in individual serving sizes.

• Eat what your pet eats - make meals that everyone in the family, human and canine, can enjoy.

• Strike a deal with your grocer or butcher. Talk to him about what you want and schedule a specific day of the week when you are able stop by and acquire what he's reserved just for you.

• Use your slow cooker. Put approved ingredients into the slow cooker before going to work.

• Involve the whole household.

• Use the pleased expression on your pet's face to energize your finding of some extra minutes daily to give him homemade food.

Chapter 4: Homemade v. Store-bought – Who Wins?

It is essential to decide on the right diet for a dog. This chapter points out the benefits, along with the drawbacks, of homemade food and store-bought food. Is one superior to the other? What are the variations between do-it-yourself and store-bought pet food? Many dog owners have contradictory views with regards to choosing the best food for their pet. These points can help to determine whether homemade food or food purchased from a store is way better for your pet.

Nourishment

Nutrition needs to be your primary concern when selecting the right food for your pet. Store-bought food may appear to be the healthiest, and most reliable option, however, many incorporate preservatives, chemical compounds and additives that aren't healthy for your dog. Don't assume all dog food in a can is junk, but you must check out the labels cautiously to help you find the right store-bought food for your pet.

Alternatively, homemade dog food doesn't incorporate any chemicals and only contains natural elements. Even so, if you choose to make your own dog food, you must be certain that it meets your dog's nutritional requirements. Both store-bought and homemade pet food can be nutritious but it's your decision which you choose to feed your dog. You must obtain the endorsement of your vet before selecting a diet for your pet.

Assortment

Homemade food has a tendency to offer a greater variety of tastes and flavors than store-bought food. Store-bought pet food generally only is available in a small selection of various flavors. If you would like your dog to savor a diversified diet, you might like to think about homemade food. You'll find recipes for a selection of different dog food and treats in the following chapters. Your dog will take pleasure in the effort you put into producing new and delicious treats and food for him to chow down.

Management

If you opt to give your dog homemade food, you'll have full control of what your pet eats every day. You can make sure that your pet doesn't eat any potentially dangerous components. If you choose to feed your dog store-bought food, you are trusting complete strangers to know exactly what your dog consumes, and based on past recalls can you really trust these companies? If control is essential to you when it comes to your dog's diet, a diet of homemade food will be the best choice.

Homemade vs. Store-Bought: Which Is More Cost-Effective?

Cooking for yourself is practically always less expensive than buying ready-made food. But, how about for your dog? Whether homemade dog food cost less than store-bought is determined by a couple of elements, like what grade of commercial dog food you purchase and what ingredients you work with to make your homemade dog food.

Processed Dog Food: Canned

The cost per 12-ounce can of dog food varies widely based on the manufacturer. A mid-range brand pet food or store brands charges around $1.25 each can. A normal premium can of dog food costs about $2.50. The price per 16 ounces for basic canned pet food is $1.67, and $3.33 for high quality canned food.

Remember that when you compare dog food rates, you can generally feed your dog a little less of the higher-quality brands and still offer your pet with similar nutrients.

Processed Dog Food: Dry

Yet again, the cost of dry dog food differs a lot with respect to the brand and grade. For midrange dry food, the price per 30-pound bag is about $35. High quality dry dog food averages $65 for a 30-pound bag. So, the cost per pound for dry midrange pet food is $1.17 per pound. The cost per pound for kibble is around $2.17.

Homemade Dog Food: Regular Ingredients

The chances are nearly endless when you're making homemade dog food. The value to make home-cooked dog dinners is determined by the ingredients you decide on and changing rates. Dog food recipes derive from a ratio of three-fifths meat, one-fifth grain and one-fifth veggie.

Homemade Dog Food: Organic Ingredients

You could decide you want to work with organic products in your home cooking to compete with the top-quality dog food brands. The value for organic ingredients is pretty much always higher.

Common Myths and Misconceptions about Homemade Dog Food

It's been a couple of years since the first melamine-related pet food recall, and in the course of that time, more dog lovers than ever decided to turn to homemade diets - cooked or raw - as coverage from potential issues with commercial pet foods. Is homemade dog food really a good preventative measure against potentially dangerous commercial foods? Sure, it can be, IF it's nutritionally balanced and accounts for your dog's breed, age, weight, activity and overall composition.

To help dog owners who wish to switch to homemade diet for their dogs, here are seven of the most common myths and misconceptions about homemade dog food. Bear in mind though that this applies to adult, healthy canines.

1. A multi-vitamin put into the meals will take care of any holes.

The issue here is this: exactly which multi-vitamin do you use? Any un-supplemented homemade diet will be short of some nutrients and loaded with others, but since there is no conventional formula for human multi-vitamins and they vary in what they consist of, just throwing one in the bowl isn't the solution.

Deciding on an all-purpose multi-vitamin made specifically for dogs doesn't always solve the issue either. These generally contain surprisingly low levels of nutrients since it's assumed they'll be put into commercial food, and they are unlikely to supply enough supplements to complete the nutritional value needs of a homemade diet.

2. Adding yogurt to my dog's food every day can help her get enough calcium.

Canines need fairly high amounts of calcium, and plain yogurt along definitely WON'T fill the gap, unless you wish to put 40 cups of yogurt in your dog's meals every day. A Calcium supplement is always recommended if you aren't feeding raw bones.

3. My personal diet is a result of a careful study of human nutrition books, and I just adhere to similar rules with my pet.

This can be a pretty typical assumption; however, it is inaccurate. Present dietary guidelines for humans aren't always well suited for dogs.

4. My doggie had some soft bowels, so reducing down on fiber will fix that.

Fiber is a crucial dietary element, and the quality of fiber you use matters more than the quantity.

In the case that your dog has soft bowels on a homemade diet, move to bland meals or trim down the volume of food by about 30% for a day or two, and look for other signs that might reveal an illness or unwanted organisms. If the issue doesn't clear up within a couple of days, speak to your vet.

5. I make use of a lot of fresh vegetables in my dog's diet since they offer a great number of health benefits.

Veggies in a dog'sdiet has become a topic of substantial debate. One approach holds that incorporating them is unacceptable, since canines are carnivores and don't need plant matter. Others stress the requirement for both veggies and fruit to improve not just essential vitamins and minerals but also phytochemicals that could shield your pet from disease.

The thing is dogs' systems tend to be more versatile than other animals and veggies provide a lot when it comes to health advantages, but once again, we're confronted with the all-important concerns, "The correct quantity of vegetables and what kind?" Some veggies have factors that may hinder the absorption of nutrients, yet others contain solanine - an alkaloid that some think worsens inflammation. Work with veggies sensibly: Minimize dark leafy greens. Green beans and carrots are often safe bets, and pumpkin and sweet potatoes are also accepted.

6. Canines don't need carbohydrates and whole grains can be harmful for them.

Dogs can' process adequate amounts of glucose from a diet composed of fat and protein alone.

What this means is that a deficiency of carbohydrates won't result in a recognizable deficit in the manner that an absence of Vitamin C in humans will generate. It does not, however, imply that a carb-free diet is advisable. The best bet is to try to maintain consistent levels so, if necessary, you may make changes.

7. A raw food diet is usually better than a cook one since canines that are fed raw food typically don't get sick.

Raw diets deviate in type; some look for nutrient balance while some use a "prey model" strategy, which imitates the diet of wolves or wild dogs as strongly as possible. These diets have grown to be massively popular over the past ten years, and to be sure, there are canines that totally thrive on them, however, some don't. As with a cooked diet, it's necessary to ensure proper formula. Raw diets have downsides as well as benefits, and may not be ideal for every dog.

Caution

Many vets, while recognizing that pet food recalls and the low quality of some commercial dog foods brings about concern, still believe that homemade diets, when fed solely, may lead to dietary instability and vitamin/mineral deficiencies that could pose risks to a dog's health. As a result, if you decide to feed your pet a homemade diet, it is crucial that you research and supply what your dog needs to remain healthy; vet nutritionists can help in creating appropriate homemade diets. While extreme care was given to provide safe recommendations and precise instructions in this book, it's not possible to calculate every individual dog's response to any food or ingredient. You should consult your vet and make use of personal judgment when employing this information to your own dogs' diets.

Chapter 5: Homemade Dog Food Recipes

Making your own all-natural dog food can often be substantially cheaper than buying commercially tinned food and kibble if you choose the right ingredients. What's more, the recipes for making your own dog food are extremely simple, as a dog's digestive system and nutritional needs are far less complicated than the human digestive system.

Some pet stores, feed stores and even some butcher stores will happily provide good quality pet meat as a base for your home-made dog food. While this meat is generally created from lower quality cuts of meat than human grade meat, it's still actual MEAT. There should be no by-products in pet meat provided by these stores, so you know what your dog is eating.

Many butchers will offer dog mince, which usually contains left over off-cuts of lamb, chicken or beef. This is often far cheaper than human-grade mince, but shouldn't contain any crushed bone. Ask your butcher if you're unsure. You should be able to find relatively good quality dog mince from most butchers.

However, dogs can't live on meat alone. In fact, a diet too high in meat protein could be bad for their health. They will need some carbohydrates, vitamins and minerals in order to stay healthy and fit.

The simple addition of boiled rice, pasta and a selection of vegetables to your pet meat with each meal means you have an easy recipe that requires only a small portion of your day to prepare. You can also prepare your own homemade kibble to serve with your homemade dog food.

Taking a bit of time out of your week to make your own dog food could also mean you're increasing your dog's health and reducing his exposure to potentially harmful chemicals.

While many dogs can deal with a range of different treats given in small amounts, some may get indigestion if you switch foods too soon or excessively. Prior to starting making your own homemade dog food, speak with your vet and ask if he / she has any specific ingredient recommendations, as some dog breeds may be more susceptible to food allergies than others. After acquiring your vet's approval, change your dog's food over little by little, slowing blending in a homemade dish with your regular food for a couple of days to a week.

Homemade Dog Kibble

Ingredients:

- 3 cups rolled oats

- 3 cups rye flour or whole wheat flour

- 3 cups cooked rice

- 2 cups dry milk powder

- 2 teaspoons bone meal

- 3 cups beef stock

- 4 eggs

• 1 cup lard

Directions:

1. Before you begin, preheat your oven to 175F (80C).

2. In a large mixing bowl, combine oats, flour, rice and bone meal.

3. In a separate mixing bowl, beat the eggs.

4. Melt the lard and mix into the eggs.

5. Then stir the egg mixture into the flour mix.

6. Add the beef stock and stir until all the ingredients are well combined.

7. Grease a large baking pan, cookie pan or pizza pan and pour the mixture into it. This is a large recipe, so you may need more than one baking pan anyway. Flatten out the mixture with a spatula or the back of a spoon and bake at 175F (80C) for around 45 minutes.

8. Try to keep the batch relatively thin, as a thicker batch will take longer to cook. It may also begin to burn on the outside, yet still be raw in the center if it's too thick.

9. The kibble should be lightly browned when it's ready. Allow the kibble to cool completely before breaking it up into small chunks.

Store completed kibble chunks in air tight containers in the fridge for up to 4 days. Any unused kibble can be frozen in air tight containers.

Suggestions: you can alter your recipe according to your dog's tastes by changing the beef stock for chicken stock or gravy, or even meat drippings. It's also acceptable to add a cup of minced chicken, hamburger or beef to the batter before you bake it.

Super Simple Dog Food Recipe

Ingredients:

• 2 pounds (approx 1 kg) minced chicken or dog mince

• ½ cup rice

• 1 cup macaroni

• 1 carrot

• ½ cup frozen peas

• 1 tablespoon gravy mix

• 5 cups water

Directions:

1. In a soup pot or large saucepan, brown the chicken lightly.

2. Add the water to the cooked chicken and break up the mince so it doesn't form clumps.

3. Add the rice and pasta.

4. Chop the peas and carrots in a food processor so they're in very small, easily digestible pieces and add them to the chicken.

5. Boil the mixture until the rice and pasta are overcooked and have expanded significantly. Stir occasionally to stop the chicken from sticking to the bottom.

6. In a small cup or jug, mix the gravy mix and a little boiling water to form a smooth paste.

7. Pour the gravy mix into the chicken and stir well.

8. Remove the mixture from the heat and pour into a sealable container.

Allow to cool before serving. Serve with homemade dog kibble. This recipe will store in the fridge for up to 3 days.

Homemade Vegan Dog Food

Ingredients:

- 1 cup dry organic brown rice

- ½ cup dry lentils

- 1 cup garbanzo beans, measured after being soaked or cooked

- 1 cup great northern or navy beans, measured after being soaked or cooked

- 1 1-lb bag organic frozen spinach, NOT thawed

- 1 1-lb bag organic frozen peas, thawed

- 1 1-lb bag organic frozen green beans, thawed

- 1-1 1/2 lbs organic carrots, shredded in food processor or chopped small

- 1/2 cup chia seeds

- 1/2 cup ground flaxseed

- 5 1/2-6 cups water

Directions:

1. Shred carrots in food processor or chop into tiny dice by hand.

2. Transfer to pressure cooker.

3. Then, change to an S-blade and process cooked or soaked beans to a medium coarseness.

4. Add to pressure cooker.

5. Add rice, lentils, peas, green beans and spinach plus water.

6. Cook for **9 minutes with natural release**.

7. Stir in chia seeds and ground flaxseed.

8. Cool and put into individual containers with tight lids and freeze for future use.

Homemade Sweet Potato Peanut Butter Vegan Dog Delight

Ingredients:

- 6 cups filtered water

- 1/2 cup whole-grain rice

- 1/2 cup black or white quinoa

- 1 cup lentils

- 3 medium sweet potatoes, cubed

- 3 cups or 24 oz. natural peanut butter

- 1 1/2 cups or 8–12 oz. apple cider vinegar, optional (Vinegar helps stop doggie gas, but if your dog doesn't • have this problem, you can omit it.)

Directions:

1. Bring the water to a boil.

2. Add the rice, quinoa, lentils, and sweet potatoes.

3. Reduce the heat and simmer, covered, for 40 minutes to 1 hour, or until the rice, quinoa, lentils, and sweet potatoes are very soft and well cooked. Stir occasionally and add more water as needed. When fully cooked, remove from the heat.

4. Mash.

5. Add the peanut butter and vinegar (if using) and stir well.

6. Place 3 to 5 servings (1 serving is about 2/3 cup*) in the refrigerator and store the rest in the freezer.

Active Dog Food Recipe

Ingredients:

- 2 pounds (around 1kg) minced chicken or dog mince

- 2 cups rolled oats

- 1 cup rice

- ½ cup pumpkin

- ½ cup green beans

- 4 cups water

- 1 cup chicken stock

Directions:

1. Place the meat, oats, rice water and 1 cup of chicken stock in a soup pot.

2. Chop the vegetables finely in a food processor and add them to the meat.

3. Cook over a medium heat until meat is cooked through. The oats will expand and absorb the majority of the liquid.

4. Remove the mixture from the heat and pour into a sealable container.

Allow to cool before serving. Serve with homemade dog kibble. This recipe will store in the fridge for up to 3 days.

Ingredients:

- 1 can sardines in oil

- ½ cup rolled oats

- 1 cup water

Directions:

1. Place rolled oats and water in microwave-safe bowl and microwave on high for two minutes, or until cooked. Allow to cool in the fridge.

2. Pour the sardines and the oil over the oats and mix together well to mash up any bones in the fish. Serve with homemade kibble.

Ideally, you should give your dog this breakfast every second day. The small bones in sardines won't harm your dog's innards, but will add some calcium and vegetable oil into your dog's diet.

Canine Meatloaf

Ingredients:

- 1 pound (500 grams) ground beef

- 1 tub 24lb (680 grams) cottage cheese

- 4 eggs

- ½ cup applesauce

- ½ cup dry milk powder

- ½ cup wheat germ

- 4 cups cooked rice

- 8 slices crumbled oatmeal bread

- 5 cups cooked oatmeal

- 1 cup shredded carrot

- ½ cup peas

- 2 celery sticks

Directions:

1. Before you begin, preheat your oven to 350F (180C).

2. In a large mixing bowl, combine beef, cheese and eggs.

3. In a food processor, chop the carrot, peas and celery finely. Add them to the bowl, along with the rest of the ingredients. Combine everything well.

4. Grease several loaf pans and divide the meatloaf mixture between them evenly.

5. Bake the meatloaf at 350F (180C) for 1 hour.

6. When the meatloaf is done, remove from the oven and allow to cool.

7. Serve cut into slices or crumbled into your dog's dinner bowl with homemade dog kibble.

Store portions in air tight containers and keep in the fridge for up to three days. Keep any unneeded portions in the freezer until you needed.

Canine Chicken Meatloaf

Ingredients:

- 1 lb (500grams) ground turkey or chicken

- 2 cups pureed beans

- 2 cups pureed vegetables (peas, broccoli, carrots, cauliflower)

- 2 cups corn flour or corn meal

- 1 cup rolled oats

- 2 cups chicken stock

- 1 cup wheat germ

- 4 cups cooked rice

- 2 eggs

- 2 tablespoons Worcestershire sauce

• ¼ cup ketchup

Directions:

1. Before you begin, preheat your oven to 350F (180C).

2. In a large mixing bowl, combine all the ingredients together very well. You may need to add a little more liquid if the consistency is too dry.

3. Grease two large loaf pans and divide the mixture between them.

4. Bake the meatloaf at 350F (180C) for an hour. Allow to cool. Cut into slices and serve with homemade dog kibble.

Put into air tight containers and store in the fridge for up to three days. Store any unused portions in the freezer until needed.

Weight Gainer Meatballs

These treats are ideal for dogs with very high energy levels that simply can't seem to put on weight!

Ingredients:

• 1 ½ lbs (700grams) hamburger mince

• ½ cup wheat germ

• 3 cups oatmeal

• 3 eggs

Directions:

1. Mix ingredients together well in a bowl.

2. Use a tablespoon to form meatballs.

3. Lightly fry the meatballs in a frying pan until they're browned and cooked through.

Allow the meatballs to cool thoroughly before serving. Give your dog two or three of these each morning as a great breakfast. Unused meatballs can be frozen in an airtight container until needed.

Serve with homemade dog kibble.

Weight Loss Chicken Dinner

This recipe is excellent for helping to control weight in dogs and should be combined with increased exercise for the best weight loss results.

Ingredients:

• 1 pound (½ kg) minced chicken

• 2 cups rice

• 2 chicken stock cubes

• ½ cup frozen peas

• Optional ½ cup carrots, chopped

Directions:

1. Place all ingredients into a large pot.

2. Pour enough water over the ingredients to cover everything.

3. Cook for 20 minutes over a medium high heat until the rice has expanded and the chicken is cooked through.

Pour into a sealable container and store in the fridge for up to 3 days. Serve with homemade dog kibble.

Weight Loss Veal Stew

Ingredients:

- ½ pound (225 grams) stewing veal

- 1 cup canned crushed tomatoes

- 1 diced carrot

- 1 small potato, diced

- 2 cups of water

- 1 beef stock cube

Directions:

1. Place all ingredients into a large pot and simmer until the meat is tender.

2. Once the meat is cooked and tender, remove any bones.

3. Cut meat into chunks and return to the stew.

Allow to cool before serving. Serve with homemade dog kibble.

Duke's Microwave Casserole

Ingredients:

- 500 grams (about 1 pound) of chopped meat/liver

- 1 carrot

- 1 small potato

- ½ cup frozen peas

- 1 tablespoon gravy mix

Directions:

1. Place all ingredients into a microwave-proof casserole dish and pour enough water into the pot to cover everything. Cover with a lid.

2. Microwave the casserole on high power for 8 minutes.

3. Stir briefly and return to the microwave.

4. Cook on medium power for another 8 minutes. Allow to cool thoroughly before serving.

Store any unused portions in an air-tight container in the fridge for up to 2 days. Serve with homemade dog kibble.

Beef and Vegetable Balls

Some canines prefer meaty treats over sweet ones. This recipe has hearty meat flavor and good aroma that all dogs really enjoy.

Ingredients:

- 2 6-ounce jars of organic beef and vegetable baby food

- 1 cup of whole-wheat flour (or white substitute)

- 2 cups of dry milk

- 1 cup of water

Directions:

1. Preheat the oven to 350 degrees Fahrenheit.

2. Combine all of the ingredients in a large mixing bowl.

3. Drop the mixture onto a baking sheet in large spoonfuls.

4. Bake for 12 to 15 minutes.

5. Allow the treats to cool completely.

Store leftover beef and vegetable balls in the fridge for up to five days.

Turkey and Veggie Dinner

This basic dog food recipe incorporates turkey for protein and veggies for added vitamins and minerals.

Ingredients:

- 4 cups of water

- 1 pound of ground turkey

- 2 cups of brown rice

- 1 cup of carrots, chopped

- 1 cup of green beans, chopped

• 1 tablespoon of fish oil (optional)

Directions:

1. Cook the ground turkey in a non-stick skillet over medium heat until the meat is cooked through.

2. Add the brown rice, turkey, and water to a large pot and bring to a boil.

3. Reduce the heat to medium-low and cook an additional 15 minutes, or until the rice is soft and tender.

4. Add the carrots and green beans and cook for an additional 5 to 10 minutes, until the vegetables are tender.

5. Allow to cool before serving.

Store extra dinners in the fridge for up to five days.

Chicken Casserole

This recipe utilizes chicken, which is a good source of protein, and plenty of vegetables to produce a flavorful mix. Green beans help your dog feel full and veggies provide vitamins and minerals.

Ingredients:

• 4 chicken breasts

• 1/2 cup of green beans, chopped

• 1/2 cup of carrots, chopped

• 1/2 cup of broccoli, chopped

• 1/2 cup rolled oats.

• 4 cups of low-salt chicken broth

Directions:

1. Take out excess fat from the chicken breasts and slice the breasts into small chunks.

2. Cook the chicken breasts in a non-stick skillet over medium heat until no longer pink.

3. Add the chicken, vegetables, rolled oats, and chicken broth to a large pot and cook over medium heat until the carrots are tender - about 15 minutes.

4. Allow to cool before serving.

Store leftover casserole portions in the fridge for up to five days.

Doggie Chili

Canines require considerable amounts of protein to ensure that they're healthy and active. Your puppy should get the majority of his/her protein from meat sources, like fresh chicken. Beans have a great amount of protein as well.

Ingredients:

- 4 chicken breasts

- 1 cup of kidney beans, drained

- 1 cup of black beans, drained

- 1 cup of carrots, diced

• 1/2 cup of tomato paste

• 4 cups of chicken broth

Directions:

1. Take out the excess fat and dice the chicken breasts into small pieces.

2. Cook the chicken breasts in a non-stick skillet over medium-high heat until no longer pink.

3. Add the chicken, beans, carrots, tomato paste, and chicken broth into a large pot and cook over medium heat until heated through - about 10 minutes.

4. Allow the mixture to cool before serving.

Store leftover chili in the fridge for up to five days.

Chapter 6: Homemade Dog Treats

Peanut Butter Cookies

Canines love peanut butter and these cookies are a great way to slip some fish oil into your pet's diet. This particular oil enhances your dog's coat, making it softer and healthier. For this recipe, it's recommended to use organic peanut butter since a number of commercial brands of peanut butter have hydrogenated oils and preservatives. If you can't find an organic one, then just make your own! For this you'll only need raw peanuts and peanut oil (and a blender or food processor).

Ingredients:

• 2 cups of flour (wheat if your pooch isn't allergic to it; white if he is)

- 1 cup of rolled oats

- 1/3 cup of smooth peanut butter

- 1 tablespoon of honey

- 1/2 tablespoon of fish oil

- 1 1/2 cups of water

Directions:

1. Pre-heat the oven to 350 degrees Fahrenheit.

2. Combine the flour and oats together in a large mixing bowl. Pour in one cup of water and mix until smooth. Incorporate the peanut butter, honey, and fish oil and blend until all the ingredients are well combined.

3. Gradually add the water until the concoction has a thick and doughy consistency.

4. Mildly flour a cooking surface. Roll the dough onto the surface to make a 1/4 inch thick sheet.

5. Make use of a cookie cutter to make shapes. Put the cookies onto a baking sheet and bake for 40 minutes.

6. Let the cookies cool completely before feeding.

Pea-Nutty Nibbles

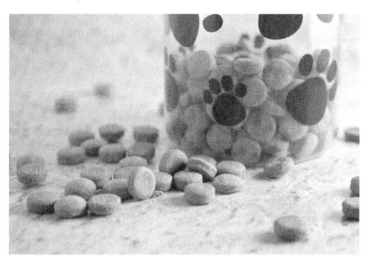

Ingredients:

- 2 cups whole wheat flour

- ½ cup oatmeal

- 2 teaspoons cinnamon

- ½ cup peanut butter

- ½ cup water

- ½ cup chicken broth

- Optional: sugar-free jelly or jam

Directions:

1. Preheat oven to 325 degrees.

2. Mix the whole wheat flour with the oatmeal and cinnamon and set aside.

3. Combine the peanut butter, water, and chicken broth, and microwave the mixture for 15 to 30 seconds until it becomes a smooth liquid.

4. Add the dry mixture and stir until you form dough.

5. Form into small rounds and flatten into tiny cookies with your palm on a cookie sheet that's lightly coated with a non-stick spray.

6. Bake at 325 degrees for 15 minutes and allow the treats to cool. Top with jelly or jam to make it an extra sweet surprise for your furry pal!

Liver Treats

Ingredients:

- 1 pound chicken livers

- 1 cup flour

- 1 cup cornmeal

- 1 tablespoon garlic powder

- 1 egg

Directions:

1. Preheat oven to 400 degrees.

2. In a blender, combine chicken livers and egg until liquefied.

3. Pour the mixture into a bowl, then add flour, cornmeal, and garlic powder.

4. Mix until all ingredients are combined, and pour onto a baking pan covered with non-stick spray.

5. Bake at 400 degrees for 15 minutes, then cut into small squares.

6. Cool and serve to your hungry dog.

Easy Cheesy Bites

Ingredients:

- ½ cup shredded cheese

- ½ cup milk

- 1 cup whole wheat flour

Directions:

1. Preheat oven to 325 degrees and line a baking sheet with parchment paper.

2. Combine all the ingredients, then knead well.

3. Form dough into a ball and roll out flat.

4. Use your favorite bone-shaped cutter to cut out cookies, and transfer to pan.

5. Bake at 325 degrees for 15 minutes, cool, and serve for tons of cheesy goodness!

Vegetarian Mini Muffins

Ingredients:

- 1 apple (cored and shredded)

- 2 cups shredded carrots

- ¼ cup plus 2 tablespoons of molasses

- ¼ cup water

- 1 cup flax seed

- ¼ cup dry oats

- ¾ cup whole wheat flour

Directions:

1. Preheat oven to 400 degrees.

2. Combine all ingredients in a large bowl. You're aiming for a thick batter; if the texture is too thin, add more flour and oats.

3. Divide batter up into a lightly greased mini muffin tins, until each cup is about ¾ full.

4. Bake for 15 minutes at 400 degrees or until browned.

Banana Peanut Butter Biscuits

Ingredients:

• 1 banana

• ½ cup peanut butter

• 1 cup oats

• ½ cup apple sauce

• 1 ¼ cup whole wheat flour

• ½ teaspoon cinnamon

Directions:

1. Preheat oven to 350 degrees and line a baking sheet with parchment paper.

2. Mash banana in a bowl, using a fork, until smooth.

3. Add the ingredients one at a time, mixing as you go; then knead thoroughly.

4. Either roll out and use a cookie cutter, or create flat rounds by hand, and transfer cookies to the baking sheet.

5. Bake at 350 degrees for 15 minutes.

Minty Biscuits

Ingredients:

- 1 cup freshly chopped mint leaves

- 2 large eggs

- ⅓ cup canola oil

- 3 teaspoons honey

- 4-5 drops peppermint oil

- 1 ½ cups flour

- ⅓ cup cornmeal

- ½ teaspoons baking soda

Directions:

1. Preheat oven to 350 degrees.

2. Combine wet ingredients in one bowl, and the dry ingredients in another.

3. Then add the dry to the wet and knead on a floured surface.

4. Either roll out and use a cookie cutter or create flat rounds by hand.

5. Bake for 15 minutes at 350 degrees. Voila—yummy crunchiness for fresher breath!

Lemon Lavender Treats

Ingredients:

- 1 lemon (juiced and zested)

- 1 tablespoon culinary lavender

- ½ cup milk

- 1 egg

- 2 cups whole wheat flour

Directions:

1. Preheat oven to 350 degrees.

2. Combine lemon, lavender, milk, and egg and mix well.

3. Then slowly add the flour until combined, then knead.

4. Either roll out and use a cookie cutter or create flat rounds by hand, transfer to a baking sheet.

5. Bake for 15 minutes at 350 degrees.

Pumpkin Peanut Butter Treats

Ingredients:

- 2 ½ cups whole wheat flour

- 2 large eggs

- ⅔ cup pumpkin puree (canned or fresh)

- 3 teaspoons peanut butter

Directions:

1. Preheat oven to 350 degrees.

2. Combine all ingredients in a bowl and transfer the dough onto a floured work surface.

3. Either roll out and use a cookie cutter or create flat rounds by hand.

4. Transfer cookies to a baking sheet.

5. Bake for 15 minutes at 350 degrees; or go a little longer depending on how crunchy you want the treats.

Chicken Jerky

The jerky is both tough and chewy, so it'll keep your dog entertained for some time. The chicken offers a beneficial amount of protein. This treat can also help to clean the dog's teeth.

Ingredients:

• Two to four chicken breasts

Directions:

1. Pre-heat the oven to 200 degrees Fahrenheit.

2. Get rid of any excess fat from the chicken. Turn the chicken on its side and use a paring knife to cut and portion the breasts into 1/8 inch thick strips.

3. Set the strips on a baking sheet. Bake for two hours.

4. Test the chicken before removing from the oven. It must be dry and hard. Allow the chicken to cool completely before serving.

Store the jerky treat in an airtight jar/container inside the fridge. You can serve this to your dog up to two weeks.

Frozen Yogurt Pops

This cool homemade treat is made out of human grade ingredients and contains fruit juice and carrots, which provide your four-legged friend an extra vitamin boost. Yogurt has calcium and protein and helps your pet break down food.

Ingredients:

• 6 oz. container of plain, NON-FAT frozen yogurt

• 1 cup of "no-sugar added" fruit juice

• 1/2 cup of carrots, minced

Directions:

1. Add the yogurt, fruit juice, and carrots into a bowl. Mix until the ingredients are smooth and well-blended.

2. Put the mixture into the ice cube trays.

3. Freeze until the mixtures are solid.

Fruit and Veggie Strips

These strips work as a more affordable substitute for the organic chewy treats available in pet stores. Additionally, they break apart effortlessly, so you can serve tinier pieces as training rewards. Fruit and veggies are abundant with vitamin C, which can boost your dog's immune system and also reinvigorate older dogs.

Ingredients:

- 1 small sweet potato

- 1 medium banana

- 1 cup carrots, minced

- 1/2 cup unsweetened organic applesauce

- 2 cups of whole wheat flour (white if your pooch is allergic to wheat)

- 1 cup of rolled oats

- 1/3 cup of water

Directions:

1. Cook the sweet potato in the microwave for 8 to 10 minutes, or until the insides are soft. Set aside and allow cooling.

2. Preheat the oven to 350 degrees Fahrenheit.

3. Mash the banana and sweet potato in a large mixing bowl with a hand masher until smooth. Incorporate the carrots, flour, and oats. Gradually add in the applesauce and water while mixing.

4. The ingredients will form soft dough. Roll the dough on to a lightly floured surface until its 1/8 inch thick.

5. Cut the dough into strips.

6. Cook on a baking sheet for 25 minutes.

7. Store leftover strips in the fridge for up to two weeks.

Apple Pupcakes

Ingredients:

- 2 ½ cups water

- ½ cup apple sauce

- 4 cups plain flour

- 1 cup finely chopped apple

- 1 tablespoon baking powder

- 1 egg, beaten

- 4 tablespoons honey

Directions:

1. Preheat your oven to 350F (180C).

2. Spray a muffin tin with cooking spray. If you can find one, use a muffin tray that makes multiple smaller muffins rather than large muffins.

3. Mix flour and baking powder together in a bowl. Add the apple.

4. In a separate bowl, mix water, applesauce, egg and honey.

5. Combine the wet ingredients into the dry ingredients slowly, ensuring all the dry mixture is well combined.

6. Spoon mixture into muffin tray and bake for around 1 hour.

7. Test whether pupcakes are ready by sticking a toothpick into the center of one of the cakes. If it comes out dry, they're ready.

Store the apple pupcakes in an air-tight container for up to a week.

Bacon Nibbles

Ingredients:

- 4 rashers of bacon

- 4 eggs, beaten

- 1 teaspoon grated parmesan cheese

- ½ cup dry milk powder

- 1 cup water

- 2 cups flour

- 2 cups wheat germ

- ½ cup cornmeal

Directions:

1. Cook bacon well and remove from the heat. Allow to cool on paper towels. When bacon has cooled, crumble it into little bits and place into a bowl.

2. Preheat the oven to 350F (180C).

3. Mix remaining ingredients together until blended well.

4. Lightly grease a baking sheet.

5. Use a tablespoon to scoop up the mixture. Drop tablespoon-fulls of mix onto the baking sheet until all the mixture is used.

6. Bake for 15 minutes. Turn off the oven and leave the cookies on the baking sheet in the oven overnight to dry them out and make them crunchy. This should create about 40-45 Bacon Bites cookies.

Peanut Butter Puppy Biscuits

Ingredients:

- 2 cups flour

- 1 tablespoon baking powder

- 1 cup peanut butter (smooth)

- 1 cup milk

Directions:

1. Preheat your oven to 375F (190C).

2. Lightly grease a baking tray.

3. In a mixing bowl, combine the flour and baking powder.

4. Use a separate bowl to mix the peanut butter and milk to form a smooth paste and then add this to the flour mix. Mix these together well until they form a thick dough.

5. Lightly flour a clean bench or surface and knead the dough lightly. Roll the dough out until it's approximately ¼ inch (1/2 centimeter) thick.

6. Cut the dough into bite- sized squares, or use a cookie cutter to create shapes if you wish.

7. Place the cookies onto the baking tray and bake them for around 20 minutes until they turn a light golden-brown. Watch them carefully as they have a tendency to burn easily.

8. Remove cooked cookies from the oven and allow them to cool completely before offering them to your dog.

Store any unused cookies in an air tight container until needed.

Gourmet Dog Biscuits

Ingredients:

- 12 oz (350g) raw liver

- 1 ½ pounds flour

- 1 cup rolled oats

- 3 stock cubes (beef or chicken)

- 1 cup water

- 2 eggs

Directions:

1. Preheat your oven to 350F (180C).

2. Lightly grease 2 cookie sheets.

3. Place the liver in a food processor and chop until it's cut up finely.

4. In a mixing bowl add the flour and oats and mix together.

5. Crumble the stock cubes and add these to the flour mix. Add the chopped liver.

6. In a separate bowl, beat the eggs well and add them to the flour.

7. Slowly add enough water to the mixture to create a firm, sticky dough. Roll out the dough so it's no more than ¼ inch (1/2 centimeter) thick.

8. Dip a cookie cutter in flour and then cut the shapes you want from the dough. Put the cut cookie pieces onto the cookie sheets.

9. Remove the unused dough portions and roll them out again. Press more shapes from the remaining dough and place these on cookie sheets. Continue until you've used all the dough.

10. Bake the cookies in the oven at 350F (180C) for approximately 1 hour. When the biscuits are cooked, remove them from the oven and allow them to cool completely.

Store them in an air-tight container in the fridge. These should last for up to 2 weeks in the fridge.

Homemade Doggie Oatmeal Cookies

Ingredients:

- 2 cups rice

- 1 cup oatmeal

- ¼ cup molasses

- 1 cup chopped carrot

- ⅓ cup spinach

- 1 ¼ cup flour

- ½ tablespoon gravy powder

- 4 tablespoon apple sauce

- ½ tablespoon vegetable oil

Directions:

1. Preheat your oven to 350F (180C).

2. Lightly grease 2 cookie sheets.

3. Mix all the ingredients in a large mixing bowl until they form a slightly sticky dough.

4. Place dough on a lightly floured clean surface or bench and roll out until it's around ¼ inch (½ centimeter) thick.

5. Cut the dough into ½ inch (1 centimeter) pieces and then roll each piece into a ball and drop onto the cookie sheets.

6. Press the balls lightly with the back of a fork to flatten them just a little. Bake your doggy cookies at 350F (180C) for around 15 minutes or until they turn a light golden-brown.

Frozen Banana Treats

After a long walk in the hot sun, what pooch wouldn't want a refreshing treat? We absolutely love this simple recipe – yogurt, banana and peanut butter. It's a frozen smoothie for your dog. Need we say more?

Ingredients:

• 4 cups plain yogurt

• 2 tablespoons peanut butter

• 3 bananas, ripe, peeled & mashed

Directions:

1. Blend all ingredients together into a puree.

2. Pour into 4-ounce plastic cups (ice trays or toddler popsicle trays work well).

3. Freeze until firm.

Can be kept in freezer for up to two weeks.

Pumpkin Dog Biscuits

Looking for a doggie digestive aid? Pumpkin is easy on sour stomachs and can help alleviate your dog's digestive issues. These homemade dog biscuits are a great way to introduce an all-natural tummy aid into your pup's diet.

Ingredients:

- 1/3 cup extremely cold water
- 2/3 cup pumpkin puree (canned or home-made)
- 2 cups whole grain brown rice flour
- 1 large egg (you can omit this if your dog is allergic to eggs)
- 2 1/2 tablespoonful flax-seed oil or olive oil

Directions:

1. Preheat the oven to 320 – 350 degrees.

2. Use two baking sheets and baking paper to avoid sticking.

3. Mix lightly beaten eggs and pumpkin in a separate container until smooth. If you don't want to use eggs then just smooth the pumpkin puree separately and proceed to the next step.

4. In a larger bowl, combine flax-seed oil and brown rice flour.

5. With constant stirring, add the pumpkin mixture to the rice mixture and slowly add water. Be sure to leave some of the rice to be used as some sort of toppings for the cookies.

6. Hand mix the ingredients thoroughly.

7. Using two pieces of baking or waxed paper, roll dough out to desired thickness.

8. Remove the top baking paper.

9. Evenly pour rice flour onto the top of the dough and lightly press it to the waxed baking paper.

10. Remove the paper and cut to desired sizes.

11. Place in the oven for 35 to 40 minutes or until the top is completely dry.

12. Cool and store in a dry plastic or glass container until ready to be served.

Conclusion

Hopefully this book has given you some insight into how simple it can be to make your own homemade dog food. You may find that mixing and matching some of the ingredients and the recipes shared in this book might suit your own dog's tastes better. As long as you remember which foods dogs shouldn't be eating, you'll find that it's easy to create a healthy diet for your dog with plenty of variety.

Aside from offering your dog a healthy diet that has the potential to extend a domesticated dog's life span, you could also be saving money in the long run.

The money you save could be attributed to paying far less on healthy, natural ingredients than you would for pre-packaged commercial dog food. However, when you add the savings from fewer vet visits for your furry friend and improved health, the benefits really start to add up.

Here's to wishing you and your four-legged friend a long, healthy and happy life together!

You've now discovered deliciously healthy meals to keep your best friend happy, healthy, and disease free! If you loved this book and your dog loved the recipes, I would be extremely grateful if you could leave a review on Amazon. Reviews are the best way to help your fellow readers distinguish good books from bad so make sure to help them out! You can leave your review by Clicking Here

If you're interested in learning how to train your dog, make sure to check out my book 'The Dog Training Bible.' It's a great book with lots of training tips for dogs of all ages! You can check it out HERE